The Ultimate Expired-Listing Guide

2024 EDITION

10-Week Marketing Campaign

Structured Agent: The Ultimate
Expired-Listing Guide
2024 Edition

Structured Agent
REAL ESTATE AGENTS WORKING SMARTER

"We believe that Success in the Real Estate Business comes from Structured and Strategic Day-to-Day Operations."

-Tim Smith
Founder, Structured Agent

Structured Agent

REAL ESTATE AGENTS WORKING SMARTER

THIS PAGE HAS BEEN
INTENTIONALLY LEFT BLANK

CONTENTS

WHY STRUCTURED AGENT?

Structured Agent is a resource hub created to help Real Estate Agents grow their business and Optimize their Day-to-Day systems. Led by Tim Smith, a 9-Year Real Estate Marketing Expert who implemented these systems to generate nearly $50 Million in Real Estate sales volume by age 25, this guide will help you **Improve your Expired-Listing Marketing Campaign** to become the stand-out agent amongst the herd of competition going for the same listings.

For Geographic Farming services and plenty more real estate tips, check us out at

www.structuredagent.com

Structured Agent

REAL ESTATE AGENTS WORKING SMARTER

OUR PREFERRED EXPIRED-LISTING LEAD TOOL: VULCAN 7

In order to effectively connect with Expired-Listing Sellers, you'll need the right tools. Our number one favorite software for obtaining accurate Expired-Listing Data, Emails, and Phone Numbers is **Vulcan 7.** If you already have an effective method for obtaining expired listing data and contact information, that will work just fine too.

- **Real-time Expired Listing Data complete with Phone Numbers, Addresses, and Email Addresses.**

- **Comprehensive owner data as well as FSBO (For Sale By Owner) data.**

- **Easily set your follow-up reminders to reach back out to your hot leads.**

For a special deal for all of our readers, feel free to use our special referral link below. Vulcan 7 will take good care of you (:

FYI: You must type the FULL link into your browser!

http://www.vulcan7.com/timothysmith

CONTENT CREATOR + CONTENT DISTRIBUTOR

CONTENT CREATOR
TO CREATE YOUR CUSTOM LETTERS AND EMAILS

Canva

If you're not already using **Canva**, be sure to download it to personalize your Campaign materials. **Canva** is a user-friendly design app that allows for lots of creative flexibility and design options. They also offer the ability to print your designs straight from the app. Though the premium version isn't necessary to create your materials for this campaign, it is certainly worth the small monthly fee in our eyes. Canva is a very powerful tool that will revolutionize the way Agents create digital and print marketing material in the coming years. **Download Canva on the App Store or on your desktop.**

CONTENT CREATOR + CONTENT DISTRIBUTOR

CONTENT CREATOR
TO CREATE YOUR CUSTOM LETTERS AND EMAILS

GetResponse

If you're not already using a great email marketing platform, or if you want one that offers more flexibility- we recommend **GetResponse**. GetReponse is a great all-in-one email marketing tool that allows dynamic flexibility in creating specific campaigns as well as organization features to effectively keep up-to-date with all of your leads. Great for keeping up with expired listing leads!

To try it out for free, scan below!

This Expired-Listing Campaign is broken down into 10 weeks. Each week consists of varying touch-points that will go out to your warm Expired Leads. Here's the broad overview:

- **10 Weeks Total.** Each week consists of Phone outreach, Email & Mail touch-points, and Face to Face conversations (Pop-bys).

- **Monday-Wednesday = Fresh Expired-Lead Outreach Days.** (Call new leads in Vulcan 7 to add to your campaign. We suggest 3 hours around lunchtime.)

- **Thursday = Warm Expired Lead Follow-Up & Nurture Day.** (Follow up and set appointments with leads you've already spoken to.)

- **Friday = Material Day. Personalized Mailing, Strategic Email, Custom Package-Drops.** (To stay in front of your Expired Prospects as they start making decisions about going back on the market.)

  "It takes an average of 8 outreach attempts to reach a prospect."

Monday-Wednesday = Fresh Expired-Lead Outreach Days.

Daily:

1. **Three hours of phone-outreach** to Expired-Leads in Vulcan 7. (Or wherever else you're getting expired lead data. You can also try connecting with your local Title Rep to see if they'll pull data for you to use.)
2. **Write down all of the contact information** of the 3 Hottest Leads you talked to during each calling session. Make sure to get their Email, Phone Number, and Mailing Address to most-effectively connect with them.
3. **Add all 3 leads into your CRM** as well as your Email-Marketing software. Make sure to put them into a group titled something like "Warm Expired Leads."
4. **Finally, print out 3 letters from Canva** and mail them to these leads at the end of the day. (Example letters for you to copy and personalize in the next section.)

PRO -TIP +

We recommend splitting your calling blocks into 2 sections. The first half, call the newest Expired-Leads in Mojo. The second half, call older leads that came off the market 6-12 months ago. The older leads typically get called less and are easier to reach. 40% of Expired-sellers re-list within the first 30 days. The other 60% wait before signing with a new agent. Make sure to reach out to both groups consistently.

PRO -TIP +

We recommend splitting your calling blocks into 2 sections. The first half, call the newest Expired-Leads in Mojo. The second half, call older leads that came off the market 6-12 months ago. The older leads typically get called less and are easier to reach. 40% of Expired-sellers re-list within the first 30 days. The other 60% wait before signing with a new agent. Make sure to reach out to both groups consistently.

Thursday = Nurture Day. Warm Expired-Lead Follow-Up:

On Thursdays:

1. **Three hours of outreach to your CRM Group**: Warm Expired Leads.
2. **Call each one of your Warm Expired Leads**. If you don't reach them, send them a text. (scripts on what to say and text templates in the next section.)
3. **If they answer the phone, your goal is to set up a time to come over** and preview the home to see if you'd be able to get it sold, or to see if you have a buyer for it.
4. **If you speak with them but they don't agree** to let you come preview the home, then you are going to send them an **Offer Letter.** (Offer Letter templates to copy and personalize in the next section). Send out 5 Personalized Letters at the end of the day to your 5 Warmest Expired leads in your CRM. Make notes and keep track of what you've already sent them and where you're at in the conversation with them.

PRO -TIP ✚

Speak to your leads as if they are your friends when you call them. Try not to sound salesy. The more effective you are at building rapport during each conversation you have, the more people are going to trust you and feel comfortable allowing you to come into their home.

PRO -TIP +

Speak to your leads as if they are your friends when you call them. Try not to sound salesy. The more effective you are at building rapport during each conversation you have, the more people are going to trust you and feel comfortable allowing you to come into their home.

Friday = Material Day- Personalized Mailing, Strategic Email, Personalized Package Pop-Bys.

---

1. **Each Friday you'll send strategic personalized material** to your warm expired leads. These are the leads you've added into your CRM but have only spoken to once or twice. In some cases you may still be trying to reach these leads for the first time.

2. **Throughout the 10-week campaign, the materials you send out each Friday to your leads will vary.** Some weeks it will be personalized print material, other weeks it will be digital touches (Email), and some weeks it will be strategic in-person drop by's.

PRO-TIP +

> Make sure you keep notes in your CRM lead profiles each time you attempt to reach them. Write-out weeks 1-10 in the notes section so that you know where you're at with each lead and which material it's time to send them.

EXAMPLE: CRM NOTES

HOW TO TRACK CAMPAIGN PROGRESS IN YOUR CRM NOTES

(EXAMPLE CRM LAYOUT BELOW)

LEAD NAME
LELAND
WRIGHT

GROUP
WARM
EXPIREDS

ADDRESS
7969 DELILAH
ROAD,
ANYWHERE, TX

PHONE
222-222-1111

EMAIL
LELAND@LELAND.NET

NOTES:

WEEK 1: **CALLED AND OFFERED TO COME DO A WALK-THROUGH OF HIS HOME. ALSO MAILED "LETTER OF INTRODUCTION".**

WEEK 2: **CALLED LELAND AND LEFT A VOICEMAIL. MAILED "OFFER LETTER."**

WEEK 3: **CALLED AND SET AN APPOINTMENT TO COME SEE THE HOUSE** ✅

WEEK 6:

WEEK 7:

WEEK 8:

SECTION 2: TEMPLATES, MATERIALS & SCRIPTS

THE FOLLOWING MATERIALS ARE FOR YOU TO REBRAND AS YOUR OWN INSIDE OF CANVA. FEEL FREE TO USE OUR EXAMPLE VERBIAGE. MAKE ANY CHANGES YOU'D LIKE TO CUSTOMIZE TO YOUR BRAND'S STYLE.

TO CUSTOMIZE TO YOUR BRAND'S STYLE AND AESTHETIC, SIMPLY GO INTO CANVA AND SEARCH "REAL ESTATE TEMPLATES." THEN, YOU CAN CHOOSE YOUR FAVORITE LAYOUT AND PASTE OUR VERBIAGE. UPLOAD YOUR OWN PHOTOS, LOGOS, BUSINESS INFO. DON'T FORGET TO SAVE THESE TEMPLATES IN CANVA FOR EASY REPLICATION IN THE FUTURE!

CONVERSATIONAL EXPIRED LISTING SCRIPT:

1) HEY THIS IS TJ WITH (BROKERAGE), I'M LOOKING FOR (NAME).

2) HEY (NAME), I SAW THAT YOU HAD A HOME FOR SALE AND IT LOOKS LIKE IT CAME OFF THE MARKET. DID YOU <u>SELL</u> THE HOME OR IS IT STILL FOR SALE?

3) IT LOOKS LIKE YOU WERE ON THE MARKET FOR _ _ DAYS.. DID YOU RECIEVE ANY OFFERS DURING THAT TIME?

4) I WAS JUST CURIOUS ABOUT WHAT YOUR PLANS ARE FOR WHEN THE HOME DOES EVENTUALLY SELL. WHERE ARE YOU PLANNING ON MOVING TO?

CONVERSATIONAL EXPIRED LISTING SCRIPT:

---

5) THAT SOUNDS LIKE A WONDERFUL PLACE TO LIVE. NOW I'VE GOT TO ASK- WHY DO YOU THINK YOUR HOME DIDN'T SELL?

6) WAS IT APPARENT TO YOU THAT YOUR PREVIOUS AGENT DID EVERYTHING THAT THEY COULD TO TRY TO GET THE HOME SOLD?

7) IT SOUNDS LIKE WHAT YOU NEED IS A SECOND OPINION AND PERHAPS SOMEONE TO TAKE A LOOK AT WHERE THERE MAY HAVE BEEN SOME GAPS IN YOUR HOME'S MARKET-POSITIONING PLAN. IF YOU COULD SELL THE HOME TODAY I TAKE IT YOU'D BE OFF TO (PLACE), RIGHT?

CONVERSATIONAL EXPIRED LISTING SCRIPT:

---

8) I'LL BE HAPPY TO BRING BY SOME DATA THAT I THINK WILL BE HELPFUL FOR YOU TO HAVE A LOOK AT. I CAN ALSO ANSWER ANY QUESTIONS THAT YOU MIGHT BE HAVING. ARE YOU USUALLY AVAILABLE IN THE EVENING OR WOULD TOMORROW MORNING BE BETTER FOR YOU?

9) SET THE APPOINTMENT OR:

BRING BY SOME INFORMATION FOR THEM AND ADD TO YOUR DATABASE IF YOU GET THROUGH ALL 8 OF THESE TALKING POINTS WITH THEM ON THE PHONE, EVEN IF THEY DON'T AGREE TO MEET YET. WE CAN INFER THAT THEY ARE A WARMER LEAD SINCE THEY WERE WILLING TO HAVE AN ENTIRE CONVERSATION WITH YOU ABOUT THEIR MOVING PLANS.

TEXT-MESSAGE SCRIPTS:

GETTING FACE TO FACE IS ALWAYS WHAT WE'RE AIMING FOR. IF THATS NOT QUITE IN THE CARDS YET, A PHONE CALL IS THE NEXT BEST OPTION. IF ALL ELSE FAILS, TRY OUT THESE TEXT MESSAGE CONVERSATION STARTERS:

1) HEY THERE (NAME). THIS IS TJ WITH (BROKERAGE), I JUST LEFT YOU A VOICEMAIL. REACHING OUT ABOUT (ADDRESS). DID YOU SELL THAT PROPERTY OR ARE YOU STILL LOOKING AT OFFERS?

2) HEY THERE (NAME). THIS IS TJ WITH (BROKERAGE). IS (ADDRESS) STILL AVAILABLE TO BE SHOWN?

(YOUR GOAL IS TO SPARK UP A CONVERSATION AND GET THEM ON THE PHONE. THIS WAY, YOU CAN SET UP A TIME TO COME BY AND SEE THE HOUSE.)

FIND EVEN MORE EXPIRED LISTING SCRIPTS AT WWW.STRUCTUREDAGENT.COM

MATERIALS- WEEK 1:

THE FIRST PIECE TO SEND AFTER THE FIRST CALL.

"LETTER OF INTRODUCTION" (MAIL)

LETTER OF INTRODUCTION

March 6, 2024

Dear Mr. Leland Wright,

I'm T.J. Smith with Christie's International Real Estate AKG, and my team and I specialize in re-positioning high-end real estate listings here in Los Angeles. We realize the importance of getting the details right when it comes to marketing a home for sale, and that targeting the *right pool of buyers* is critical to achieve a timely, top dollar sale.

We've become familiar with your property since its previous listing on the market and feel sorry that it hasn't yet received an acceptable offer. However, this result is not uncommon. Even highly attractive properties go unsold when positioned sub-optimally on the market. When your timing allows, we'd be happy to come by and share how we believe your home could be positioned more effectively to a pool of best-fit, qualified buyers. Often times home-sellers will alter their moving plans altogether when their home comes off the market unsold. We hope you'll find that this doesn't need to be the case with a more thoughtful and targeted approach.

Feel free to reach out when the time is right for you and we'd be happy to share resources, data, as well as thoughts and ideas.

Best regards,

T.J. Smith

T.J. Smith | Aaron Kirman Group
Director, Listing Re-Launch Division | AKG
Christie's International Real Estate

PRO TIP+

ESTABLISH YOURSELF AS AN EXPERT IN LISTING RE-LAUNCH

📞 310.488.1728   📍 433 N. Camden Dr, Beverly Hills CA 90210   ✉ tj@akgre.com

Recreate our letters in Canva. Feel free to use our verbiage!

WEEK 2: THE SECOND MARKETING PIECE THAT YOU'LL SEND YOUR WARM EXPIRED LEADS.

"OFFER LETTER"

OFFER TO REFRESH YOUR
HOME'S MARKET LISTING

T.J. Smith
Listing Re-Launch Specialist
Christie's International Real Estate, AKG
433 N. Camden Dr, Beverly Hills CA 90210
310.488.1728

March 19, 2024

To Mr. Leland Wright-

Kindly accept this offer to allow us to provide you with a complimentary assessment of your home's previous listing. This no-pressure sit-down will allow you to pinpoint areas that were lacking in your previous listing's strategy. We will explore your home's positioning, depth of exposure, and how it was angled on the market to determine why you did not see the result that you were after.

We specialize in re-positioning homes on the market that were previously listed but did not sell. Our specialized approach follows a carefully crafted sequence of targeted marketing strategies based on 120 Data-Point Parameters that expose your home to the entire pool of buyers that are the most likely to write an acceptable offer on your home. We've found through our experience that a successful relaunch of a property begins with figuring out where the mark was missed the first time around. Feel free to reach out anytime with questions. We are happy to help.

Best wishes,

T.J. Smith | Aaron Kirman Group
Christie's International Real Estate
Listing Re-Launch Specialist

📞 310.488.1728
✉ tj@akgre.com

"EXPIRED DATA POSTCARD"

T.J. Smith
Listing Re-Launch Specialist
310.488.1728
tj@akgre.com
DRE 01991986

3 Reasons Why Your Home Is Not Selling

Not Targeting The *Right* Buyer Pool

Your home is not for everyone. Showing it to the wrong pool of buyers is just a waste of time. Success begins with a carefully crafted targeted marketing campaign that will expose your home to the most likely set of end-buyers.

Suboptimal Positioning

How does your home stack up against the others that are on the market? Hiring a team that knows how to position your home where it fits best and shows best against similar options on the market is vital to success.

Lack of *Meaningful* Exposure

Every Agent exposes your home to the market by listing on the MLS. However, it takes a carefully sequenced & targeted marketing campaign that casts a net from various angles to the individuals that are most likely to write offers on your home.

Staying top-of-mind while your prospects are in the decision-making stage is absolutely critical. We'll send subtle material like postcards and informational emails between the more personalized material in order to not overwhelm our leads.

Pro-tip +

"THE KNOCK-DROP"

JUST
SOLD!
—

123 Anywhere St.
Any City, ST 12345

$1,695,000
Courtesy of Agent X

TJ SMITH

T.J. Smith
Listing Re-Launch Specialist
Christie's International Real Estate
310.488.1728

RECREATE IN CANVA. FEEL FREE TO USE OUR VERBIAGE!

What's a Knock-Drop?

A knock drop is when you create a single "Just Sold" flyer for a recently sold home in your expired lead's neighborhood. Make sure to credit the agent who sold the listing on your flyer and as always, check with your local marketing laws to be sure you're compliant. You're going to drop by the Expired Lead's house with the flyer to share the news with them. The goal here is just to get face to face with them so you can have a conversation about their moving plan.

"LOCAL FOOD REVIEW EMAIL"

(THESE GET ENGAGEMENT)

The last 3 pieces your leads have received from you have all delivered value without asking for anything in return. After this week, we will ask for the meeting again now that they are familiar with who we are. Don't forget, we are still reaching out to them by phone each week on top of these materials that we're sending them.

WEEK 6: THE SIXTH TOUCH, THEY KNOW US BY NOW.

OFFER LETTER #2

Couple this with a text or a voicemail. Give your lead a head's up that you've sent over an offer letter regarding their home and ask to set up a time to discuss. We've been nurturing them for 6 weeks now and they are in the decision making zone.

TJ SMITH

OFFER: COMPLIMENTARY
PRICE AND MARKETABILITY
ANALYSIS OF YOUR HOME

T.J. Smith
Listing Re-Launch Specialist
Christie's International Real Estate
433 N. Camden Dr, Beverly Hills CA 90210
310.488.1728

AKG | CHRISTIE'S
INTERNATIONAL REAL ESTATE

March 26th, 2024

To Mr. Oppenheim:

Kindly accept this offer to allow us to provide you with a complimentary assessment of your home's previous listing and current marketability. This walk-through will allow you to pinpoint areas that were lacking in your previous marketing strategy as well as some great ways that your home could be positioned to generate top-dollar offers.

We specialize in re-positioning homes on the market that were previously listed but did not sell. Our specialized approach follows a carefully crafted sequence of targeted marketing strategies that expose your home to the entire pool of buyers that are the most likely to write an acceptable offer on your home. We've found through our experience that a successful re-launch of a property begins with figuring out where the mark was missed the first time around. Feel free to reach out anytime with questions. We are happy to help.

Best wishes,

T.J. Smith
T.J. Smith

📞 310.488.1728
✉ tj@akgre.com

RECREATE IN CANVA. FEEL FREE TO USE OUR VERBIAGE!

Pro-tip ➕

Instead of just sending this to one Expired lead at a time, send it to multiple leads at once to save time and to track which pieces are getting the most opens and interaction.

LA Real Estate News

UP TO DATE ALL YEAR LONG

Does it make sense to re-list your home in 2024?

There's reason to be optimistic about home sales this year

With rates down to the 6% range and below with certain programs, homebuyers are looking at an affordability increase of almost 20% from 2023's interest rate peak of 8% back in October.

Coming off a shaky '23: Where are we now?

Homeowners, investors, and real estate professionals alike experienced quite an ugly year last year on the Real Estate front. Many opted to take to the sidelines until market conditions smoothed out. A combination of rate hikes and greater economic inflation created a significantly less affordable home-buying environment, slowing sales pretty dramatically.

However, 2024 is off to a promising start. The fed has announced as many as 4 rate-cuts for the year. Historically, when the fed cuts rates, Real Estate activity picks up. Here's what we're starting to see..

LOS ANGELES REAL ESTATE NEWS

Does it make sense to list your home in 2024?

What we're seeing so far and what to expect

Home Prices - According to the 2024 National Housing Forecast, Los Angeles home prices are projected to climb 9.2% in 2024. These figures land LA in the Top 10 US cities for Real Estate Growth this year.

Inventory - So far in January & February, we've seen an increase in inventory of around 17.2% in Los Angeles. We anticipate a further increase in inventory as we move through Q1, Q2, and Q3, likely pulling back as we near the election. We anticipate a bit of market stall around election time, which is the usual case.

Interest Rates - There is no crystal ball in Real Estate. However, general sentiment is that rates will continue to drop this year, resulting in increased buying power for homebuyers. As we've watched rates drop from the ~8% range to the ~6% range, home sales have picked up considerably. We expect to see a ~22.9% increase in home sales this year.

Is it the right time for you to list your home on the market? Set up a meeting to discuss.

T.J. Smith
Christie's AKG
Listing Re-launch
Specialist
310.488.1728

WEEK 8: "UPDATED ESTIMATE OF VALUE"

PIECE #8: MAIL A CMA. (COMPARATIVE MARKET ANALYSIS)

Use your preferred CMA generator and print up a Comparative Market Analysis for your Expired-Lead's home. In the package, include a personalized letter letting them know that you just wanted to keep them up to date on their home's value.

WEEK 9: "5 STEPS TO PREPARE FOR RE-LAUNCH" (EMAIL)

As we close in on piece 10, we want to remind them one last time that we are the Listing Re-Launch expert and that we're here to help guide them through a successful sale. Piece #9 serves as a gentle reminder of who we are and what we do before we attempt one last time at a final offer.

5 Steps to Prepare Your Home for Re-launch

In 2024

T.J. Smith | Christie's International
Director, Listing Re-launch Division
310.488.1728

Assessment of Previous Listing
In order to identify precisely where the mark was missed on a previous listing, we conduct a thorough assessment of your home's exposure on the market as well as its positioning in relation to other similar listings.

1.

Identify Target Buyer-Pool
Your home is not for everybody. That's why it doesn't make sense to mindlessly market it to everybody. Rather, we hone in on the pool of buyers that are consistently buying homes most similar to yours in the neighborhood.

2.

Build Positioning Strategy
How your home stacks up against the others on the market is important. We carefully identify your home's strengths and weaknesses against the competition to position it accordingly so that it's the best option on the market.

3.

Targeted Coming-Soon launch
Basic human psychology knows that people want what is just out of reach. We target our network of ready and able buyers in a *coming-soon* teaser campaign that highlights your home's most special features.

4.

Sequenced, Targeted Exposure
80% of buying decisions are made after the 5th consideration. We keep this key data-point in mind as we build a carefully crafted, sequenced, 120- parameter marketing campaign to keep your home in front of the buyer's eyes at the most optimal frequency.

5.

Ready to get started?

WEEK 10: "POCKET LISTING OFFER-LETTER" (PERSONALIZED LETTER)

The final piece of the campaign. This piece is sent as a last-ditch effort to get behind this listing. After you've called this expired lead every week and shared all of the campaign material with them and they still won't budge- one last offering to market their home as a "Pocket Listing" has proven to be an effective measure for getting our foot in the door with sellers.

"Off-Market" Marketing Proposal

Dear Fabiola,

I'm T.J. Smith with Christie's International Real Estate. My team and I do a great deal of business by marketing homes "off-market" to our internal pipeline of ready-buyers. This means that we are able to get homes sold without listing them on the MLS or doing any open houses.

We do this by sharing the details of the property with clients that we are already working with in order to find interested parties.

We're reaching out to you since we have seen your property come off the market. If selling your property is still your goal, we would be happy to market it within our brokerage with your permission. Doing so is as simple as snapping a few quick iPhone photos of the house and gathering some details to share with our buyers. If this is of interest of you, give us a call and we will gladly get to work.

If you're not interested in this, we are sorry to bother you and wish you a wonderful day. We hope to talk soon.

Best regards,

T.J. Smith

T.J. Smith | Christie's International Real Estate
Property Re-list specialist
AKG Beverly Hills
310.488.1728

📞 310.488.1728   📍 433 N Camden Dr, Beverly Hills CA 90210   ✉ tj@akgre.com

If you've signed a listing agreement and are working with an agent on your property, please disregard this message.

CLOSING: THE #1 RULE FOR SUCCESSFUL EXPIRED-LISTING CAMPAIGNS:

CONSISTENCY AND FOLLOW-THROUGH!!

THE AGENTS WHO ARE THE MOST CONSISTENT IN NURTURING EXPIRED LEADS ARE THE ONES WHO GET THE LISTINGS. EVERY WEEK YOU NEED TO GET YOUR MATERIAL OUT AND HAVE THE CONVERSATIONS. AFTER YOU'VE GOTTEN THROUGH ALL 10 WEEKS WITH LEADS THAT HAVE NOT RELISTED WITH YOU YET, YOU CAN ALWAYS START THEM BACK UP ON THE ROTATION OF MATERIAL AND OUTREACH. TRY NOT TO GET TOO ATTACHED TO LEADS- NOT EVERYBODY IS GOING TO WORK WITH YOU AND THAT'S JUST THE NATURE OF THE BUSINESS.

YOUR NET-WORTH IS YOUR
NETWORK

JOIN US: STRUCTURED AGENT +

⟶

ELEVATE YOUR AGENT NETWORK
AND EXPAND YOUR REFERRAL
BUSINESS AS A MEMBER OF
STRUCTURED AGENT PLUS: A SUITE
FOR VIP AGENTS WHERE WE SHARE
WEEKLY MARKETING MATERIAL,
TOOLS, AND MARKETING TRENDS.

SCAN TO JOIN:

YOUR 5-STAR REVIEWS MEAN EVERYTHING

YOUR 5-STAR REVIEWS ON AMAZON MEAN MORE THAN YOU CAN IMAGINE..

SO MUCH SO THAT WE ARE GOING TO SEND YOU <u>2 BONUS EXPIRED LISTING SCRIPTS</u> IF YOU LEAVE US A ROCKSTAR REVIEW ON AMAZON👏👏👏

TO LEAVE A REVIEW, SCAN BELOW. SEND US A SCREENSHOT WHEN YOU'RE DONE AND WE'LL SEND OVER YOUR SCRIPTS!

Thank you!

www.structuredagent.com

Made in the USA
Las Vegas, NV
28 September 2024

95914597R00024